T0208538

Push Prana

Pushing your potential through poetry

Jason Allen Pace

authorHOUSE®

AuthorHouse™
1663 Liberty Drive
Bloomington, IN 47403
www.authorhouse.com
Phone: 833-262-8899

Published by AuthorHouse 11/23/2021

ISBN: 978-1-6655-4465-8 (sc)
ISBN: 978-1-6655-4466-5 (hc)
ISBN: 978-1-6655-4467-2 (e)

Library of Congress Control Number: 2021923496

Print information available on the last page.

This book is printed on acid-free paper.

Contents

Chair

Walking slowly tip thrillingly on the toes I stare
Silently departed from one of the 5 senses caring I am aware
Must I retire for my legs are in dire?
Need of a rest
So must I contest?
Sit is of a commence in time complete,
I'm still standing tho
Wondering contemplating with a rock of my body
to the right now a lean to the left
Legs bend in relief now sit down is met
These arm rests feel good and smooth almost silky against the elbows
Curvy like an S at the fingertips kept
Plush to the touch of buttocks much
Its red velvet with a fade of yellow on the outline...
Don't sit so awkward a still voice to me whispers
I scoot forward just a little so calm is of an acquittal
I twitch at the sound of vibrations chill
My head turns quickly as I slouch to the right for real
A hand rests on my head
Sit up straight! I hear again
A flinch commences and I do listen
As I sit up straight comfortable is blissful
Crossing my legs with the right knee on top
Left pointer fingertip is resting on I mean scratching my lip
Right forearm is on the already bent knee commit
Head is tilted upward as my eyes squint slightly
I am immensely relaxed now...

Biceps Superb

Grip tightly now with a grit teeth growl
Encase the fingers around a metallic mass
Oh wow!
Massive it's about to be
The transforming of bodily compliance
Grip tightly more is the impending alliance
It's a tangible caress of careful assurance
A twist with precision and deep breath of passion
The countless amount of looks is stern envious cashing,
Approve that form and lift to the movement of slow speed contour
A tickle is felt from hand to arm
Then beyond
A muscle contraction and wow of alarm
The raise to completion is a yea to a twin muscular satisfaction
Feel it tighten
Skin moves to a swell flexible with winding rivers flowing
The blood rushing of a knowing
Indicated by a raised pipeline of vascular living,
Downward the movement slow with a two sided comply
A double feel of satisfactory euphoria of burn commences why
Biceps scream immediately piercing muscular ears
This awesome journey contributes to a bodily comprehend...

Widely Latius

Look and position the hands slowly then grab
Turn the eyes upward look for a grip grab
Position again and breathe
Feel the gritty ridges on this bar that's about to enhance a need
Stationary depicts that which steady knees appreciate,
A movement behind the head renders sensational tone abate,
A stroke down to the back of the neck
Feel the sensation of tone filled curvy
The muscle is relaxing and I feel no complain
Moving on up is the weighted feel of no blame
Another downward pull and the arm feels queasy
Upward slow release relaxation is pleasy,
Breathe now on the pull down makes the shoulder muscles burn
The lower back feels a fullness and its a stability adjourn
One more repetition is an obvious inevitable...
A quick pull quicker than before
Momentum powers up an isolation's viscosity implore
Travel straight does the bar as arms bend more
Slow to the top touch of trapezius tense
An upward movement slow control makes so much more sense
Cardio control will discipline the muscle burn conditioning
Release the grip of both hands for it's of releases compendium
Blood pressure is lowering as palms gain color and composure
Brought by the release of a silver weighted exposure
Breathe deeply in and out for easy next set closure ...

Breastplate Strong

Lying in wait and muscles are tense
Hands do grip the weighted pleasure of bent
Bar type ready
A ninety degree press made pleasingly steady
Arms sway to a steady stabilize commence already ready
Oxygen fed for life does depict
Arms extend slowly as hand tightly grips...
Forearm muscles bulge a curvy simplistic
Back presses into a support for your support diaphragm constrictive
Stability ushers in a confidence of expense
Arms are extended now almost completely as air from lungs commences
The weight is lighter now,
I let out a split-second sigh from a weight room high
Well more like a grunt
Some just witnessed an impressive stunt,
Gravity whispers raspy please bear with me
For your benefit I'll just push steady some slightly against thee
So, I take a deep breath in as gravity commits
Chest balloons much so then triceps tighten as arms are bent...
Lower the extend again as confidence begins
Again
Creating muscularity so repeats are akin to a win...
Bench press now this cadence of correct
Bench press again now the chest expand is met
Breathing on the out while feet are flat and steady
No lateral lean of bar, it's resting on a metallic lip safely
Cradle this sigh of relief for one set is now completely...

Press More

Reaching gripping this off the rack balancing
With the other hand the same equilibrium is here for the blaming
Sit down on that bench now!
Wiggle body to stabilize the weightiness of proud
Knees are now bent
Slowly the right arm then left arm engages and readies the swing
Laying back with weight over the chest shoulder width seem
With one notion of a motion the pectoral isolation is at hand
Commitment is stand
Looking to the ceiling for some hope of bland
Pressing to the extension and wobbly is sublime
Wobbly meets strengthy stable forearms
Follow that imaginary line and perpetualize the norm
Keep it correct
Proportionality is for the pectorals though not too fast less exercise is scorn
Stabilize the push for this poundage is moral
So are the eyes that gaze upon thee plural
Dumbbells are returning to the chest to touch once more
Split second only
To press once again this cardio weightiness creates sin sweaty sore
A vein becomes now more visible on the sweaty forehead
Pumping iron makes the iron rich blood excitingly led
The pulsating heartbeats of gently abiding
Just two more sets make hard bodies inviting...
Feet are resting on the edge of bench as chest engages
Back is flat as onlookers strike amazing gazes
Set up check the mirror for next in line is an array of multiple praises...

Squat Thrust

Stiffen the arms and stiffen the torso too
Gluteus crunch in line with the torso of muscularity construe
Leg muscles tighten akin to a fullness blend
A straight line is drawn and plank position is of the absolute contend
Body structure is strong while fingertips are tense
A deep breath in for the toes haven't engaged since
A push of the floor is next with a quick hop context
Knees are at the chest now
Momentarily
They almost touched a split second is mesh
Back to the plank hold,
A wonder of how many
The matter is that seconds depict sweaty is plenty
Exploding the hop quickness quickens with wow
Back to the workout and work grind is now
Eyes on the floor focused until quick crouch comes around
With a glance at self in the mirror wait for a reset of composure compound
Push to the plank with a continuity of exposure
Sweat worthy is the comprise
Feel the build of body wise
Quads are at a fullness to the touch
Hamstrings are screaming that this isolation is too much
Gluteus feel the burn of interval weary
Another thrust and the countdown is of comparing now completely...

Three Times Push

As I grab a weighted contraption
I raise it in a manner of praise
Straight are the arms of a stationary presence
Elbows are locked at an inwardly measure
Amaze is the gaze of onlookers pleasure
Eyes look into a world of back at you over sizable,
Do it right or render no optimum over resultful
Just that of plenty plus the plusful...
Must muscles suffer a time related sore without optimum implore?
Lower the weighted pleasure as palms are facing each other more
Press up the weights and enable the breathing
as you enter an elongated territory,
Twist that pleasure and feel the burning of muscular
tissues displaying isolation's pleasing worry...
Multiplying optimizes primordial issues
The breaking down of this is creation's infinity
Oh yeah oh yeah
Oh, yea to the everlasting already
Bring down the weighted grip of constant speed confetti
Accomplishments being hit from more than one angle
Let not the naysayers be that of an entangle,
Listen then hear the inner canal of air traveling abode
Building up to the outward explode
It is now a push breathe implode
Of perpetual intervals commencing an interesting node...

Full Leg Exposure

Sitting feet positioned width wise of a shoulder shrug composure
Toes pointed a northward and eyes are too
Gleaming of what's next
Sent from me to myself it's a momentous self fulfilling text
Legs are at a ninety-degree angle and I'll not falter
Leg muscles are tense to the point of a burst ready press
Think not less
Ready the press
Feel the tense of much more when the seated slot
is a modified downward implore
My mind says press now this weighted pleasure and so do I
Muscle tissues commence another tense
This interesting slide of a glide offers accomplishments
of a repeatable comprise
Confidence rises as weight does too
Making the next time's session a greater ado,
Lower the weight steady now
It's isolation's passion
Feel the burn in the quadriceps this is the hamstrings compassion
As metallic plates stack it's a muscular inclusion
Ready press again
It's a calf and hamstring work tandem akin,
As you stand up you feel a gluteus fullness
A tightness that'll soon be your isolation newness
You feel a slight ting
It's a burn sensation sing
Fat cells are screaming harmoniously in agony of this sting
In time recognize silence for their death is beneficial
Transformations commence to a thoroughbreds' essential…

Lunge Press Again

Right step forward out to an extend
Heel presses first then toe with a blend
Balance
Stationary creates a quadricep feel and wow
The back-knee creeps closer to the floor
Stop
Time equals how
Pulse press equals isolation sublime
Torso is still now and it's waiting for a break in time
Heels are tense and toes are ready
Raise hips up and down please keep it steady
It's a humanistic metronome perpetually already
Hands on the hips for another movement commence
When concentrating the balance is real easy to watch
Time release from a deep breath in
I can do that!
Onlookers look then follow the consequence
It's a suitable portray where professionals have prevailed
Onlookers can tell where wisdom shines well
Self-sufficient continues where the mirror does fail,
Another step and the torso is straight vertical as well
90 degrees is prevalent as both legs are steady
Press down the press up
Pulse down explode and feel the erupt
Up to the toes and down to the heels
This modified lunge is a nervous thrill
A longevity euphoria of a flourishing feel...

Wrist-able Curl

Bend those knees and steady the heels
Sit the gluteus way back rest forearms on knees and chill
Palms are faced downward while gripping the weight in mind
Steady thyself and rev up the engine
Is it this time you mind?
Angle the wrists upward until forearms burn well
Repeat the concern until learn is tell
Hold
Now muscle build is combined with a contour fiber swell
The forearm sculpture is a continue of mold
Watch the ridges bend until a bold statement is sold
Rest and complain if you must
Now rev the engine again
Isolation moves up thru forearm muscles past the elbow bend
On to the biceps now for they peak like a mountain's ridge
Relax and twist the wrists
Watch the muscles react like rolling hills as a river of life runs thru them
Around the hills winding higher then disappearing only
to reappear when a mountain's peak is re achieved
Now do you believe?
Hamstrings and legs are burning also feeling the building of achieve
Calories following suit for they are burning too
Wrists twist to a rev zoom and forearms are brute anew,
Slow then fast is also an interval's passion true
Isolate the cardio for fat blasting thrashing....
Twist the wrists more even curl them now and feel the strength
no time now for isolation crashing…

Side Raise

Eyes glaring into the distance
At your own face front feature
Legs are straight and arms hang long
With light weight in hands the gripping is strong
Shoulders are tense ready for the shrug commence
Breathe thru the nose and hear it howl since
Arms are rising both in unison
Carrying the load higher over space and time in dire
Need of control
Now keep it slow
Teeth gritting a growl and it's heard intensely so
Arms raise even higher with concentration of bold
Giving praise as the head tilts slightly back with control
A smile abides for strengthening is of attract
A peak appears on the shoulder from no lack of the workout attack
Holding for a second or two now slowly the arms lower
Even though isolation comes quick keep lowing the slower,
Sweat drips from the small beads on forehead gathered
Feel the latissimus bulge ridged with a sweat shine lather
Thru a trimmed-up shirt with an underarm cut,
Shoulders peak like the Rocky Mountains once again
The jagged protruding and such
Arms are straight like boards
love handles tighten with a blend
Benefiting body and soul
An hour glass mentality is mend…

Chest Fly

Semi sweaty hands floating slight freely in front of head
Over the chest is in between while lying on the back is no dread
Hands are heavy like concrete while fists are strongly made
Outward is a lateral arm direct of a 135 degree bend of shade
Trust the speed and slow is much making isolation a just
While moving out feel the pectorals flex wider and you're breathing much
Stretch out to the point of uncomfortable
Don't stop until the feel is real
Full range is met of a compromised form set,
As I look to the right a weighted hover is seen
A look to the left and concentrate is mean
Back muscles tense to a timely release
When movement upward is of an imploring increase
Arms are straighter as they get higher
Pectorals squeeze as weight tapping is closer
You're just getting started
So let not thy motivation be dearly departed,
Why are chest muscles nearly startled?
Repetitions render a bumpy appear on a shirted chest carded
The mountainous relevance is not that of a feminine appear
Though they come so near
Steer close to peer
Attempt to touch
Payoff is much…

Climb the Mountain

At the plank position breathe and hold
A straight line is drawn from head to toe
It is so
Ready the knees and feel the blood flow
With a quick thrust of the right and left knee in tow from the waist below
A touch of the chest was almost of the know
With every thrust switch there was a feel of a twitch
Muscle fibers of the gluteus bloat and the skin does stretch
Skin tight pleasures emerge with a threat
Offering on lookers a feel of regret
When and from where will their self-motivation come quickly to the surface?
Hopefully quickly from the landscape of humanistic lustfulness,
At the plank toes are nimble
Perfectness is the symbol
Quick interval taps to the floor before knees drive in are continual
Simple breathing is the release while push more is passionate able
Palms are flush to the floor and it's a grit teeth nose snarl implore
Eyes are focused then relaxed even some more
Attention to sweat is dripping galore,
The measurement thereof puddles of fore mentioning
This climbing creates contoured abdominal tension
Rest assure that timely benefits are the kindly intention...

Cliff Hanger

Steady the plank and breathe in deeply
Breathing in slowly feel the lungs fill with air
initially coursing thru the nose canal
Slowly imploding into I'm climbing this mountain now
It's a side concentrating endeavor over steep edges and weather
Steeper still with abdominal thrills steady that
torso conserving breathing until
A slight pause at a proper plank
Singular alternating knees bring in a movement of soft toe tapping slant
Sweat drips from the forehead while quick movements are kept
Worthiness asks the question are you ready to level up the step?
Raise that right hand and stiffen the plank
Don't stifle the sturdy less quiver is stank
And don't let the sharp edges of the cliff render a slip
Fill the lungs with air once more and stiffen the grip
Now breathe out and hang freely for stronger has won,
What comes next is an alternate grab needy of fun
Pressing forward is a ready momentous understatement
Breathing intervals of concentration calm
Let not thy forehead drop less compromising form is done
Keep eyes focused overhead as elbows pump to the beat
Let not slow remind of hindsight retreat
Rocky edges are now a blur for time has made easing
Cardiovascular capacity leaping has caused a creating of pleasing....

Up Jump The Uppercut

Take two steps quick and wide
Left and right knees raise them high
Keep the feet wide now hands just punched
I sigh
For the legs know how to abstractly move and why
Thighs tense up as shoulders round through
Bringing the elbows to tap the knees anew
The quick tap is accompanied by an inward explode
That gestures to the abdominal area for it's time to implode
Feet hop closer than farther apart
Right and left hands come to an overhead clap
Aggressive is the shadow of jumping jacks about
A hop in between renders a sliced-up roundabout
Of a punch that's only chin high that's packing much might
This speed too is a powerful instep to the music pursue
Somewhat searing into the body's subconscious
Anticipations' euphoric just cried with joyousness
Brain wavy auroras eliminate muscles fatigue
The outwardly tension is sore no need
For more
Since toning is of an amazing curvy galore that hot Bodies adore
What's more in store but a happenstance abstract of uppercuts implore…

A Standish Cycle

Upright and shoulder width the feet are positioned
Arms wide in praise while fingertips are spread conditioned
Ready for the movement for the toes are elegantly pointed
Sighted ahead the eyes are staring
They look down to see that knees are bending
A sigh of relief has just been sent
Conscientiously standing now ride that bike ride it
It's visual at best so twist that torso twist it
This standing is demanding so quicken that motion quicken it
Elbows touch the knees to criss cross the affectionate
Slowdown that movement to enhance the correction
It's a short tap to the floor and toes move quickly
Add that bounce and squat
A standing up resets the election of weakly...
Another repetition is that of goodness
The flow sweetness of this is sweat worthy of soothing
Elbows to knees again feel the float of elegance
Fast then slow so watch your step and the middle below
Directly below the tightened torso
Keep steps wide and so that another elbow to knee is the appeal of glee
It's abdominal isolation's benefits upright
These standing bicycles are completing me completely...

Bicycles Lying In Wait

A stretch of the arms
The legs are freely stiff and straight
With a deep breath in the nose
Theirs a ready to let it out slow
Fingertips feel the ear lobes
Tickle
Another breath in and out
The instigation feel of this is something of a fickle
The elbow moves right toward the knee left
Touch and ready the switch quickly and keep it in step
Multiple controlled movements render sweat worthy pleasures
I'm lying my back against the floor
This relax is of a momentous worthy pleasure
What measures does prove rightly for an abdominal burn?
Cosign this time and watch these movements of beneficial earn
Benefits continue when exercises do
Why does this complain reek of construe
Crunch again and feel a possible plateau of ado
With fingertips to the back of head
Elbows touch to the knees anew
This is not a sin
Even though others think of it as a burning sensation akin
Ride that bicycle
Ride it
Reap the benefits until others witness the results
Of slow and fast made to last
Longevity is continue and true…

Heels to Heaven

With the back against the floor
Eyes are raised high
Focusing on ceiling tiles contemplation and why
It's easier on the neck just you wait and see
With a concentrated squint yea that's a focus ability of glee
Hands resting by the lats and gluteus
Both feet are raised slightly in unison
Breathing in the diaphragm the heels are stabilized crucially
Heels to the ceiling and press
Heels release and press
Heels to the ceiling and press
Raise the gluteus and press
Hands help to stabilize the tired and fatigued balance
Realize the raise
Now create the release
Reps render an amaze which exonerates a brain wavy haze
The high is much at hand and it's a clear clap demand
The plan is of a step up worthy pleasure
Tap the heels to the floor its operation is leisure
Even though legs feel heavy and the abdominals are cramping
Sweat drips from the tongue which is uncontrollably a workhorse stamping
Through concentrating passions hands rest on the hips
Are you holding the legs high maintaining a balanced grip?
Take a deep breath inward and contract it now
Breathe out and lower the legs slowly
This is performed with very little doubt
Isolation and slow movements create not a clout…

Vertical Planking

Steady thyself
Now sturdy is the wait
Head is in line with the butt combined
Legs find the line and it's straight thru and thru
Release the tension
Breathe in as the body moves a downward plank pursue
Nose momentarily touches to the floor so make it lightly touch
Breath outward as the push is much,
Plank hold and control it momentarily
Release again only when must is easy
Quicker is such but keep the butt on lock
Line up the body this time for benefits of lot,
Body lowers to energy's conserve
Body now moves upward to muscles converge
Tighter still is the chest as it contracts
Bigger still is the frames' structure intact
Stout is present at interval's rest
Rest more to press more it's more stoutness of next
Arms bend from a relaxed contend
Pectorals stretch to a tightened blend
Contoured and full felt is the muscular cleavage
Picture your silhouette pumping joy into the psychic believer
Picture the pumping up of onlookers likely,
The pump pumping of present
Futuristic muscular chest fury
The pump pumping of present
Convinces a positive outcome of stout worthy's jury...

Heel Raise

With my back against the floor and my eyes raised high
Relaxed is a plenty and I'm about to know why
With fingertips beside the thighs
Feel the soft cushion of exercise stability
Breathe in and out feel the abs expand convexly
Breathe in feel the abs contracting a demand
Raise the heels two more inches and stabilize the command
Breathe in and hold it
Feel the burn
Keep the heels there and don't beware
Release your fear of isolation's stare,
Release your fear of no can do
Seconds more will depict a lower back and abdominal reap of benefits ado
Prepare to sue me
While your benefits witness me smirk with glee…
Hands to the ceiling then fingertips to the head
Raise the heels again while push pulse is the thread
The lower abs and lower back strengthens
And oh the wow and how
Time says it's about time
So muscles harden like lead
A flourish of heat treated happiness hints that there's no time for dread,
The exercise is easier still for time proves it a worthy appeal
More time proves even easier the ultimate implore
Stronger still and stronger more
Steady the raise
Stronger implore…

45 Degrees

Focus ability raises an awareness and the thighs tingle
For they're about to move
Quads tense as blood rushes thru veins of ready pursue
And muscles have nowhere to hide
As you breathe inward lower back is engaged
Heels raise to a degree of 45 amaze
Steady the sturdy of tenseness worthy
Breathable nostrils are controllable already
Conditional expand of lung capacity steady
Renders the leg raise easy and ready,
A swift concentrate let the right leg implore
Concentrate more and let the left see what's in store
Concentrate and alternate feel the burning of lower back sensation sensible
Wait one minute
Well just a second
It's also the feel of abdominal equate mating
Faster the cardio
Get it now
Push breathe in to the let it out wow
A flourish of euphoria powers the constant
Raising the expand of conditionals kept
These leg raises are much easier now
oh yes much easier now...

Toe Touch to The Plank

Standing at an attention
Hands are ready and the back is too
The bend is ready for you and I to do
Legs are straight and so I reach
Slowly downward toward the floor fingertips do creep
Eyes are now focused between the legs
Fingertips touch the toes as they are encased
Symbols depict stylish footwear
Walking are those fingertips now
Along the floor outward and oh how the abdominal isolation is wow
Body moves to a straighter implore
Holding and hovering the gluteus squeezing while you're breathing
That air is moving along nostrils follicles teasing
This is controlled with a feeling of serene
Small breaths are seen as conditioning has
commenced so now I'm ready to convene
Abdominals improve their sculpture while a contracted diaphragm is intact
Concentrate exact
Fingertips move the body toward an A frame erect
On until a bent is formed at the toe area correct
It's a toe touch of such
A lingering over the shoes I can feel the blood rushing to my head
Back muscles move like thick rubber bands
You push and they pull while standing up straighter is now
Pushing harder now you're stronger so let not
your back move like worn out rubber
What a good thing this is a soft still voice whispers
TT to P it's easy you see
TT to P and then some and oh how it's very easy to be…

Three Times the Press

Grip the weights and heartily commit
Fingertips are at a shoulder width presence
Steady position for the left side and steady the arms too
Ready are the forearms so move them to a ninety degree improve
Feel the muscularity burn like wow
After a threesome of contract-able conversation implore
Press against graivity now winning-ness is met more
Stationary those arms and twist turn the hands
Slowly descend and feel the burn from awkward movements akin
Press again and don't wait for it's a burn time commencement
Many times more is isolation' contentment and
seven times over is a brush of the clover
Exercising is right so feel isolation's fatigue of might
This is four times lucky so much so it balloons muscle fibers skin tight
The sight able envy onlookers have pupils of greenish awe
Well since that's the case get thee from over there to over here and plan a turn
Push thyself until properties include a tricep burn of isolation urn
Something way more than what you feel now it's
creating your being of they say so wow
Balance the work ability of exercise efficiency compile
Equilibrium is now achieved so celebrate increased believe
Increase the push and feel the respect of plenty
Time renders tic toc of silver-plated reward
Watch how the reward congratulates excellence toward
Wisdom just decreased the interval time and
longevity is on reserve and it's so sublime

On slightly bended knees press forearms up then release
On bended knees press and let sweaty palms increase
Steady muscles are aware of the steady upload of stress
Press breathe and let triceps burn with sculptured pleasure no less...

Pull The Wide Grip

Standing with a double hand sturdy straight arm salute
Grab and take hold of a metal substance wide and bold
Hold the hang of the body in balance
Pull is ready and commencement is the challenge
With palms facing the face, fingertips are grip worthy
Biceps bulge too so hence is the hurry
Tense are the arms
How wide is your width?
The body now raising steadily isn't the myth
Chin is in line with the bar but that's not enough
Pull a little harder over the top is much
A now holding briefly is for soul pleasing of such
Controlled releasing proves a slow motion easy
Elongated hanging is a recharging of teasing
Breathing out slowly is the ultimate completed now
Let's do it again subliminal voices say to me
Let's do it again in unison now let us calmly see
How will it feel if the body raises quickly again,
The chin reaches and body releases perpetually it's a contend
Repeatable passion renders strength content
Repeatable passion renders bodily wisdom no relent
Repeatable more renders stoutly galore…

Dips

Hanging in air and balanced at the moment
Fingers grip tightly at the sturdy of atonement
The tangible tone curvy muscular keeps the body momentarily unmovable
Shoulders are tense as chest shifts forward
Torso lowers and knees do too
Feet are crossed to symbolize a screw
Arms are engaged as low gets lower
Pectorals stretch to an isolation peel as the fat burns more or
When multiple reps feel breathe able convey,
Pushing the requirement for restart is ready
For this time lower depicts speed more pretendy
With every stop then start knowledge and wisdom is gained
Mind gets stronger with no time for complain
Oh how the smarter workouts are there for the gain
A build more is present when the combined technique is thrill
Let not a glance in the mirror cause the triceps to shrill
Proper form is now a sculpture of heal
I think I'll increase to more reps for real
The resulting in longevity muscularity is true and real...

A Movement Held

Hovering over space give me more time and space
Breathing deeply in through the nose
When air comes out the mouth I hear
The sound of a subtle howl and light tickle on the lips so clear
So I smile a bit for this interesting happening
The diaphragm has been engaged as aware is breathing
From head to toe a line is drawn
From head to toe form is shown
Oh so correct is the shivering and shaking of burn
Abdominal learn
Pleasure concern
Knees release and touch the floor for an awesome interval relief of burn
Engage never leaves when commencement governs the knees
Abdominal tenseness stays true to confirm it's the
learn to an elevate of muscles discern
Realign those knees up off that floor!
Next level is now a condition implore,
Rock back and forth to enhance the mood
Rock back and forth alternating nose to floor and oh it's crude
Or where the fingertips are at least
Holding a perfect plank of power and peace
Do you feel the pulsate of heart happily?
Do you feel the quiver of results resilience?
Gratitude is oh so very near
Gratitude has now exonerated all nearful fear…

Side Plank-able

Ready set and lean to the straighten body confirm
Remain for the stretch that learns the concern
Of right then left now loop the return
How many reps will it take to reach the impending burn?
A slight wait for a while into a moderate twist turn
Feel the goodness of elongated torso stiff adjourn
No injuries tomorrow or today for this time is
very needful for a conscious concentrate
I'm breathing with a conscientious created controllable mate
This body that has leaned to the side is a shoulder fatigue of bold
Oblique intrigue
Let not thy legs wiggle with ease
No succumb to a drop for that move is a representative of lethargy
I just felt free to compromise this smooth concentrated exercise
I feel so relaxed now
These enhanced planks has created a wow...

Quicken The Jump

The impulse of pedaling those revolutions quick worthy
The impulse of the foot cycle smooth and steady
Push firm the platform of firm already ready
Still steady now is the form of corrected a plenty
That's knees inward and pointed straight forward
No over correctness less the joints succumb to fatigue
Slow breathing with the torso diaphragm engaging
Quadriceps tense to a full feel of amazing
A slight raise of the torso
Legs are straight to the point of comfort
Gluteus are moving back to the seat now
So go ahead and control the touch
Make plush the seated of gluteus squeeze so much
Speed depicts how much dripping there is of salty goodness
Brought about from a cardio penetrating meekness
Time depicts when motivation will rule with honor
Is that from syllables vibrating around harmonious arrange?
Where are those aggressive one liners of high octane?
Cycle the time when legs engage the raise
Of gluteus from the seat steady
Repeat the remain until burn worthy is sustain
Complain to a contrive now hover is the same
Repeat cycle loop
I hear that results say the same,
Skin tightens from muscles built so strong
Can you hear that?
Results are saying the same...

Stationary Jog

With a lift from the cycling to engage quadriceps now
A hover in between the saddle and jog what a wow!
In time with musicals
It's a constant harmonious pace
Stay tuned for what's next
It's an awesome case to make,
Tunes bouncing inside a mind that's willing to unwind
Feet moving to the motion of no out of control combine
Seated with a passion with no shoulder side to side lean
Just a push of much feet worthy
The resistance of such is not that much swervy
Concentrate hips sternly,
As my eyes observe the hips stationary presence worthy,
I feel the burn commence
I hear a voice inside my head coaching me
Which leads me to a momentary standing hence...

Speed Train

Starting slow
Very slow
Pushing against a slight resist
Keep it constant while seconds pass
It's time to increase cadence's persist
Loop the keep and cadence increase
This constant crescendo redundant at least,
I can feel the revolutions of pedal-ism get easier
Now I'm faster as I settle in to a cardio briefer,
A sprint is commencing
The speed is at your capacity
Seconds pass as you erase the complexity of your over indulge of exhaustion
Slowdown is now to muscle up the train of a faster educated itch
Feel the muscle flow while hearing the musical twitch
A cadence settle again is preparation sweat worthy
I'm faster now and you are too
This cycling is easier now which has created a jelly muscle feel ado…

Looped and Committed

Thoughts congregated to a proving of likable motivation
Sifting and comparing through the addition of possibilities
An exercising that might leave one momentarily different
Different as in good
A betterment of embodiment,
The immunity of height makes a strong structure of vascular muscularity
Binding the cells,
It's an exhales' purpose
Time plus supplementary renders unlimited intellectual muscularity mobility
A squint of the eyes is indicative of muscles tense
A mind well focused with lips curled in grit
This is an advocate of determination commit
An embodiment of benefits reaping submit,
Onlookers commence a concentrating cradle
This curls the earlobes and makes concentration debatable
This note taking is careful
Must I commit when others do not?
Every time overtime proves wisdom of a lot
This knowledge of a got
It's from pages of past into belief not destined to rot
But love with a purpose that is looking back to learn,
Another seal of commit that's craving for more learn...

Revolutions Worthy

What's worth the time?
Is it a cycle of substantial?
What's worth the sublime?
But an overcoat of results and warmth of repeatable,
From the right leg feel the pedal of moving instability
Moving the toe into secure please pull the straps tightly
Left foot is already for the ready of pedaling steady,
With a full turn of the knob rightly
Resistance renders a burn and time begets the isolation's yearn
Shoulders moving side to side in unison to the sound of the beat
Pedals move with revolutions of a constant cadence keep
Amusement is not of a recovery
It's a warm-up to work
Motivation seeps a gradual and positive covert
Crescendo speed says to me chronologically
I'm keeping you a little while longer,
So release pleads with intervals
Hence is the happiness of replenished marvel
An embolden of the soul
The body does now behold
When work comes again a heighten capacity unfolds
Making it look easy it's an onlooker's woe,
Hear the drip of sweat onto the tile beneath
Listen to the breath
Now you're breathing with ease
A heart palpitating calm is happily a please
Revolutions of pedals easy is a calculating tease...

To Strengthen the Stretch of an Educated Stride

The resistance of the tweak has no room now for release
In time again renders another stretch begin
The difference from pavement to grass and to graveled dirt
Lets the legs feel the burn of a resistance made hurt
With a lean forward and push
A slowdown is short lived,
I just traded slowdown speed for the burn and
what a turn it was for isolation's learn,
Standing high and resistance is at about a seven
The bouncing is controlled and speed is irrelevant
Hands grip the handles so calf stretching is benevolent,
Peddling comes to a slow stop
Toes are pointed upward
Legs are straight and locked
A sit back is slight
Dropping elbows is blight for the calf burn is now slight...
Back to cycling now and 30 more revolutions is the demand
I need more results and I want the fullness feel command
So therefore I don't stop
For I crave the burn and mirror reflect appeal
One more revolution is presently for real
Again, the burn comes near and so I feel
That the strive forever is the ultimate deal...

Breathable Palpitations' Terrain

With a push stroke of the pedal and we're off
It's into a land of opportunities and they are possibly challenging
What exercise lies ahead of what I know not of?
End result reveals that of a build capacity of such
It's a graveled path riddled with muddy ruts
Just ran into one
Coming out of it is wet and dirty even though concentrating is some,
A push cadence commences of pedal since
Realizing becomes more that easier is bliss
Along the way I'm learning of techniques harp
A slight slowdown now for that curve was sharp
Right into an uphill battle over rigid gray rocks
I'm positioned into a zig zagging,
Onto the next
My foot just bounced off the pedal and then back on
From the aforementioned rocky path
Quadriceps are continuously engaged
Now I'm swerving to survive the maze
I must jump now and so I did
Fast momentum in technique was needed
around that dangerously sharp bend
For if not
The hard-uneven ground would be a tragic contend…

Initiated and Motivated

The thought of standing before anxious eyes
The onlooker's anticipation of the impending comprise
Ready to critique if presenting wasn't wise,
From the very first time asked was made manifest
To the time when reply cried a sigh of yes,
I'll do it now so why have I waited?
A butterfly effect must have mated with berated...
Gazing upon the onlookers
It's a step to the stage commence
No time for backing up
Delivery must be mint and met with commit
Something very tasteful of workable submit
It is!
With love in tow it's a sweat able exhaust
Propelling forward the results of exercise juggernaut
Burn felt now is of a naught
A fullness of feel and strong is the appeal
a rest that isn't ill is very benefical
Still more is when a rest isn't ill...
Brainwaves causes the vision seemingly seen through someone else's eyes
The scent says this was an experience of an authentic positive high
Felt for a first time
A hook able adventurous body awareness comply...

Flapping Subcutaneous

Tickle is the feeling when nauseous consummates livers' uneasiness
Peering into curious eyes that are awaiting and
debating for knowledge increasing ties
Tick ticking
The time is closing on a building up to delivery's unwind
Self-checking upon an indicator's suspense
I feel the rising of flapping commence
I feel them fluttering from side to side so much
that torso doubling over abides
There's a lingering in the middle so when will I recover?
Suffer now and that's okay for I'm stronger than before
So, the doubling over decides it's not worth compromises comprise,
So rise is to the occasion
Slowly the flapping slows to a slow flutter
Tickle becomes faintly while fluttering becomes faulty,
A steadfast shoulder shrug is the release of a stiff legged combine
So now walking is that of cartoonist sublime
With a quick shot of confidence some of these butterflies retreat with no play
Now ready portray and project a feature artistic display,
Existentialism commits to the creating of atmospheric belief
Bodily movements improve with time
It's the structure and integrity of human's composure incline...
Another flap in the stomach and it's okay
I'm now immune to butterflies perpetuating display...

Observable and Elated

A glance across an area of embodiment elate
Sighted complete of believe able sedate
Movable flanges
They're restless with anxiety
Propriety leans toward commencement night
Saying I'm ready right now for a sweat worthy alright,
It's a user friendly of a modified muscular no deny,
Moves depict that of what they want and why
That's more moves of isolation taunt
More movements coax breath able subtle enhance wrought,
A heart felt glance with a smile is purposefully a dance
Watch out for slippery spots of happiness splash,
In time there is a look toward circular's clash
The project that tells of a time that my mind objects
Of a coming quick when the end meets met
But for today
I must make quickly an elated complete
For now clockwork is the being of our happiness bleak,
Bodies sweat and burn thru tic tocs and so
Minds loose time for the caressing musicale so bold,
A smile comes and goes and comes again
Hmm that's bless
Let not the next be that of a mess,
Down to a stretch and smiles remain a chuckle and reach
Facial subliminal portrayals hint exercise benefits of contain and teach...

Heat Treated Territory

It's a push play already with a stroll to the forefront
Mirror images crisp and bold
I see a standing curvy intimate,
Again and again
In tune and tight like a clockwork of an atomic,
Mannerisms are vibrating with critiqued forms anticipating
Tonic choreography vibrating of iso-obtain while muscles
contract and quickly remain Perpetual contain
Movements move easily and It's a visionary's pleasure remain,
Awkwardly the turn of events become consciously aware
Awkwardly the faces depict attractive compare
Sweat makes attractive glisten akin
No impedance now of a complain depend
That's okay for its overcome with gain of blend
Muscularity thinks I'll keep pushing until
Muscularity mates burn with isolation thrill
Hold on now and just wait for muscular fullness is of the obtain
Traveling over a strong curvy embodiment where straight edges did claim
The passenger seat ride is smooth and serene
The eye box is filled with a soothing sight from all this hard work
Sweat salty drippy is happily to the point of proving,
Landscape is rolling beautiful with all kinds of cuteness
This territory is now favorable and this living is priceless…

Isolation's Protege

Holding the delightful and weight filled benefits of muscle fiber intertwine
Slow creep is the seep of release filled cortisol combine
The tension is growing as muscles contract
How light was the weight that's about to prove might
It's not
Concentrations' correct has built a skyscraper of trained
The towering over cowards of frail buildings wane
Slow and controlled was the architecture abstract
Conscientious times of wisdom compel exists until the next was well kept
Movements depict a sculpture that's more eye box pleasure than laziness sore,
Another slow moving seven count of concentration uncover more
Look upon thyself to create good form and make it shiny polished like chrome
That's about to be hard like concrete and sculptured like granite
Hence comes that which lifts the status to that of a planet,
This body is of a magnificence that others dream as synthetic
But in reality,
Authentic has created and constructed a core indescribable and
indestructible of muscle fibers twist tied to implore....

Abdominals Abnormal

Mindset ready so are you ready for the task?
A purplish euphoric is dancing timidly
Facial expressions are questionable alike while lips twist a turn to a curl
Eyes twitch up then over to the left
How much time is left up to the inevitable buildup?
Muscle twitch commences are about to be abound
Around the room circling so feel the feeling of astound
Over time abnormal has been made a type of normal
But normal to some it is not
A look around again it's who and how many?
Oh, one more just walked in,
In unison bodies lay and legs move to a beat
A torso tuck just made diaphragm contract breathy without a cheat
Small sweat beads form tickling the forehead bleak
Never fear for this bleak is optimal and beneficial,
More time has elapsed and more than the masses have appreciated
More benefits continue so much more than the onlookers can relate
Bystanders beware and become so intrigued
Step to the pace of now be around and become a
part of abnormality's capacity compare
Continue,
Push breathe once more into a deep breath with a controlled purpose
Think through and through until obscurity is in the unobstructed rear view,
Hands are raised with arms straight out to the side
Raise them a little higher and breathe in and out once more
Do you feel it?
Omni euphoria is abnormal so many times,
That it's just now became a normal comprise…

Constructed Impulse

Rushing bodily and kinetically thinking
It's a slow potential that's push breathing completely
You're about to see,
The results of hearts racing and livers quivering
It's not what you think but you're about to see
A check of the time piece for time is slipping presently
Steadily keeping conscientiously
Is it now time for a slowdown cognitively?
Not so for people need thee
A walk just turned to a trot as the heart rate increases
The sound of a heart beat gets faster and now it's stronger pleasingly
This step and workout is to the tune of a hard-hitting beat
Why does my heart flutter when I'm at rest?
Anxiety lovely is at its best
Walking thru the door way of stress relief carelessness
It's a conceptual build to make comfort more comfortable
Wait for it now let's do it
Okay we're doing it now
The exercising exercise that the comfort zone makes wow
Not me but you
This atomic skyscraper we just built is a massive comprise
Days just got squeezed into seconds and that
was an awesome experience surprise
Materialistic makes spiritualistic appreciate to a point that's wise
A sharpened response so the body responds
Onlookers smile
The self feels younger while it's a beget of stronger
It's a sigh of relief while the lifestyle becomes fulfillingly longer…

Constricted Impulse

A twitch tilt with a turn of the head
A flourish of a conscientious thought felt dread
A split second discern to enhance the embodiment
Opposite to the opposite and no alternate yet
Breathe out on the push
A full extension is met
As push becomes greater it's an exercise of range readiness kept
Endurance quickens as fatigue whispers of course
No more shouts for the fatigue's voice box is squeaky hoarse
Completion more makes endurance a more quicken of the sort
Constricted over rules where the alternate had made user friendly
Results are mediocre
Repeat are many for the benefits of the same
Same is one sided and concentrate is remain
Containing a genre which says wait your turn
Other side says I'm ready so hurry the hurry
Tomorrow will let you see muscle soreness while aware is blurry
Feel the benefits pulsating mirror worthy and flurry
Sight sensitive is the benefits and they see them now
On you
They wish to themselves that they had the one-sided twitch
A clench of the teeth is believing that concentrating is bliss...

Caffeinated Calm

Hmmm
Wondering what the next thought just might be
Wondering when the positive thoughts might become thought easy
Fingers twist the plastic softly to free the ultimate hydration
Raised to a height of a tilted back refreshing elation
Emptying into a body presently depleted
This free flow is complying to moist mouth not deleted
Forceful is the usual
Concentration control makes meditation bold
It's a self-observation indication of time worthy display sold
Anticipation fuels anxiety's wrought
Heart rate quickens as euphoric fills the mind taught
The cognition's mandate is fueled with divine
Cells ascending of a brain wave filled depending timely unwind
Intake measures are of how many
The interesting higher of euphoric build plenty
I feel lighter now and so the thrill
From side to side things move slower still
Like the swaying of trees before the storm in slow motion
These bodies sway too
We're maintaining the grip of a sturdy pursue
And oh how calm am I....

Aggression Dissipated

At a stature of ready-made commencement confrontation
The building of emotional and radical atonement predication
Moving into place its dissipation's purpose
So
I slide and slide laterally until squared up meets abide
So
I eye and eye until the concentration with good form is about to comply,
The elbow presses away from the target atone
Oblique contractions are torso twists alone
The building of power that's about to release,
I'm driving my fists into a leather substance at least
Creating an indention that some call an abstract crease,
Giving thanks now for the blood pressure and stress release
Onto the other side to even this out
Pressure release continues grit teeth worthy about
Muscles tense to the point of hurtful anxiety
With every touch of leather tough
Pressure releases with greater much
Feet switches movements from front to back
Power increases the aggression intact
Power increases as aggression produces the diminishing of stresses on attack…

Formidable Pressurization

With a concentrated hand position let not weights be the guide
Be thee the guide no matter how heavy the weights abide,
Holding weights to my side I now raise them to a height of 90 degrees comply
Steady is the weight and so wait is no lie
Pulse press repeat until cue says no more
Lower slower until the relax is implore
Raise up from the wait now post a 90 degree formidable
Constant keep the speed of repetition elongate complete able
Reach over the head and hold hover remain
Lower the weight down while concentrate is to blame
Shoulders are aware of their momentous stability potentiality
And they are now most definitely a kinetic of isolation true
Hands reach further back to the point of reverse muscle contract
Now push upward now
Universal exercise techniques with good form are now
tickling the benefits of longevity wow…

A CC Concentration

Squinted transparency
Eyebrows arch to a point
Nose snarls to a growl sniff while lip curls inward for a lick,
Fingertips tap the chin while concentrating eyes are lifted
The body is calm equipped
A warm chill fills the area between the right and left hemisphere for real
Lingering
Body shifts from the force of spiritual winds blowing
Mouth curls to a positive gesture of knowing
What comes next just might please the pleasure
The pleasure of pleasure that measures the measure,
Strolling through time and definitely thru space
The pace has now quickened
The bending of surroundings as aurora maneuvers the blending
Carefully
The imply comply and reply of embodiment
The questionably onlooking of onlookers for understanding is wane
As they complain for not knowing how and
why the calm with you does remain
A caffeination flows then permeates the brain
Tantalizing and saturating the synapses' kinetic contain,
I'm floating over still waters now
A cool brisk wind tickles my brow as supersonic thoughts slow to a creep
A perpetuated caffeinated calm is now…

Awkward Powerful and Positive

This doesn't feel right for I haven't been here before
This doesn't feel right for no one else does an implore
With an exercise like this
Why does the turn of my arm make my mind quiver?
The hand grip is adverse as muscles start to shiver
From an elasticity burn it's a concern of churn
Muscle fibers twitch from the drink of isolation's urn
Results reveal positive now I yearn for more isolation,
I'm stern
This doesn't feel right
So positively I correct the awkward now the awkward is stern,
This doesn't feel right although I still learn
This doesn't feel right so now why do I adore?
Results say because of me don't you see
Transformation has commenced as it smiles with glee,
This doesn't feel right
Powerful is the movement
Breath with thought quickens as results prove improvement,
An awkward powerful exercise
Confuses muscularity positively purposeful
Awkward is now in the right direction of convenient affection
Awkward now resides in a powerful and positive commonplace...

Two Kicks

Running is modified and kicking back is correct
Keep those arms pumping in unison direct while opposite is met
Legs do follow in a situational suit
Eyes are straight forward as the torso is too
Concentration makes the reverse kicking more beneficial in might
Double that speed of leg movement and remember the goal in sight
A double kick to the right gluteus then same on the left pursue
A ruffle to the shorts is momentary with no wait for abide this time
A salty substance is dripping onto the floor below with control
Now the body feels that a plateau is in tow
The body dances such that both legs are moving similar
Arms quicken with the pumping upon every existing breathable
Fingertips are steady
Palms are facing each other with fingertips apart
Stay alert and alive let's thrive on this cardio abide
Looking around the room
Some bodies are steadier than others
Power heel kicking makes up for lagging composure,
Lean forward and let thy eyesight touch the floor
May you be tuned to the wood strip lines of galore
Let your movement coerce with the musical beats
No stopping until self-satisfaction is agree…

Runner's Stance

On your mark get set set set
On your mark get ready ready ready
Set it up and don't you wait
Set it up and contain the hate
Transform the hate into motivation sublime
Maintain the mate of positivity divine
Disperse it into power takeoffs' purpose
Disperse it into the gut of stress diminish
It's a stomach jab and quick fist plunge,
Legs twitch from anticipation
Sudden movements readies fibers of elasticity
into a flux of idled pulsating power,
Rocking back and forth
Shoulders slightly raise into a "I don't know why"
Glancing at the ground then an upward look of sigh
Eyesight lines up with destination front wise and futuristic,
Nostrils move up down and side to side quite altruistic
A ready-made grimace comprises
Calves tense as glutes do too
Left arm swings into chest at a ninety degree fingertips are open anew
Right arm straightens out directly diagonal behind oneself
Momentarily levitation compromises a power-up
of power take off comprises...
A fine-tuned ready set to run this race is wow...

I Don't Know Why

As arms hang neutrally beside the body weighted
They're preparing for a movement that might render the neck jaded
"I don't know why" becomes the anthem of exercise scream
Now concentrate the comply
I sing unto myself loudly
So loudly
That others look upon me questionably but undoubtedly
Momentarily
Until the exercise feeling says to them" I don't know why either"
"But I love this so much"
So much still until the repeats justifies such,
With arms straight down beside the body
The shoulders are steadfast and they're waiting and pondering
Until movement says unison now
Steady leaves steadfastly in the moment of evolution's concentrate
"I don't know why "is said faster as isolation's
crescendo depicts sweat beads capacity
Oh, how careful time depicts a shrug worthy comply
Up then down more times than this to feed the wow
Hold the hold then roll the sway
Repeat the shoulder roll until relax is intact
Now it is that "I don't know why"
Knowingly turns into "I surely know why now"…

Sigma Sequence

Numbers fall in line
Marching to a beat
They're steadily structured and quite precisely complete
Carefully measured and fed at the right moment
When depleted there is a hesitate then reinstate with pleasure component
The measure decreases as composure increases
Creating strength and stability releases,
The form filled contour muscles ting with delight
Speed driven concentration helps meditate with might
This is an exercising quickly so the body becomes
hardly softly but curvingly solid
A model of what's to come is even more sculptural embodied
These exercises are getting easier now
That's what I say while benefits are a burn less wow
Now the rest of this is lame
It's going quickly now while the benefits remain
A burn some more
Just a little bit more
Sets of these exercises depict a push breathe commit sore
Now slow up that rep
Even slower than that so isolation is kept...
Continuing this now until single sequenced is met...

Hot Yo So

At an exhausted stature that fingertips do adore
The touchy tangible of sticky elastic was bore
This class consists of sweaty stretches that I find pleasurable
With eyes focused underneath the heat-treated pressure of atmospheric dry
Why am I not so dry?
Soaked territory does depict with a left hand on left knee
This is bent so much it represents a modified committed be
Soaked with a wet saltiness
A sniff of the shirt
Sigh
Comply I have with laziness so I do much deny
A drip from the shorts soaked to the point of soppy
A plop and I hear the connection to the floor beneath me
So now is the mat darker from this interesting happenstance
With a drink of a cool substance makes cool down now a chance
Sipping on hydrated twice oxygen drool
The throat is dependently at ease a soothe,
On to the next kinetic heat-treated happy time
On to the next nourishment of sweat worthy norm
I'm now walking thru the door of exhausted calm adore...

Sunrise Shenora

Peering over waves to where waves meet the sky
Standing on a softness positioning feet to become
more comfortable with comply
Now they dig into the ground and I feel more at home now
Steady is the stance of appreciating relaxes wow
As the wind moves around and thru the body elated
It cools where sweat once met dripping related
Only dry heat was present as a concentrated abode
Causing a reaction traction of elevated index woe,
Wind hits the iris
There's a squint then a smirk
This is what dreams dream while making one think of a hurt
A glint shimmer and a bright shine is seen
It's a hit to the forehead of heat happiness of now no complain
Wind is much warmer while elated is still
The rise of higher more heated wind will
Stand to be reckoned and hang around until
Clouds say stand still and the moon behaves for real,
Gravitation weakens while ocean waves twirl slow
An aggressive wave pushing decreases to a small beach ripple abode…

Seaside Sensations

Peering from afar it's a look over area space
This proves to be a scene of a relaxing sedate
Choppy wetness depicts a wave forming delight
from continuous wind blowing,
A heat-treated surprise
A stiff legged stance
Eyes squint to sun's bright controlled rays
Wind lifts the shirt curtail to a flip flop array,
A turn and walk minutes later and I see another scene of happy portray
It's me standing on a creme colored softness making feet happy with glee
Peering out over waters
Eyes are squinted with the nose disgruntled as air permeates the body
This is what I need
Drops of water plops me in the face as choppy waves
move from moon's gravitational disobey,
As I look up, I see that clouds are scattered
Clouds are still moving from the trade winds' purpose matter,
I could stand here all day and clear
I could stand here all day and smile
The mind is much clearer now
Uncontrollable positive thoughts make me go wow...

A Decreasing into Muscular Excellence

Fast flowing and maintaining at a high-altitude pace
Capacity renders that of athletics' intensity silhouette trace
Bringing more energy completely
A charismatic choreography of muscle-bound strength is presently
Intensity kept until tic toc makes it well known
It's time to release now for an appropriateness has been sown
A decent quick form is filled with a much needed apparent attempt
Strategic says the concentration with perfect
posture shall not be kept in contempt
Results are worthy of nickel sized eyes that don't squint until
Amaze has subsided,
Slow reps now and nose breathing is a must
Fast moves were broken now exhale conquers much
Allowing for a distribute able power to be efficiently wrought
Isolation makes the mood a contouring smile sought…

Descending Discernible Muscular Vascularity

Starting with a platform of a statistical count
Staying until complete is segment sound amount,
Decreasing isolation announces makes for an efficient body enhancement
Form filled and controlled less equates to an excellent announcement
When pause has no power over segments implore,
Seated position is how you sit
Torso of a 45 degree should be your concern-able commit
Hold and how long will determine just how you are fit
Fingertips caress slightly the lower abdominal area commit
Elbows ready for a task of merely twisting admit
Now touch the mat and tap it there
Return to the center is a lean back aware
Breathe in and breathe out
Will make the other side compare
It's easier now but I'm still aware
The isolation of this makes teeth grit a dare
A bead of sweat drops from the ear lobe to the shoulder
I leave them there for more is about to become bolder,
Even when sets get smaller the feeling of a burn
sensation contends with fatigue
A blending of isolation with one more repetition is beneficial of glee…

Hour Glass Repetitive

Like the gathering of a mind ready to combine then unwind
The thoughts so profound when meditated upon the more depicts a sound
So syllablistic quiet
Now the body depicts
One on a mission to sculpture the riff
Mind you
These movements are grouped together in line and so
constructed in a way it makes the body yearn
For the next time
Now on to the next the body reaps divine
Results of this kind makes the body look more like a heavenly design
Comparable to you and me
Repetitive movements grouped together gets
shorter as calculated moments pass
Intensity remains
Burning is insane as a pause is appreciated with clockwork the same,
Transition quickens to the point of manifest thought
Relief realizes an evolutionary agreeable wrought
Down to a singular moment of movement,
On to the next and it's a doubled exposure provement
Exercising is additional like a perpetual in step soldier
To a gain increasingly abide-able
With every increasing comes complain undecidable
For insane isolation burneth with passion
It casually contains an increasingly benefits' cashing
To before sculpturing an hourglass deplore
From repetitive implore
A sigh breathes easy now from an hourglass initiative thought process core...

Predict Depict and Substantially Entertain

Head is tilted sternly while eyes are focused forward
Mind shifts gently as exercise synapses sparks to a flicker
Body moves as mind subdues to harmonized twitches making muscles coo,
Vocalized reminders to clairvoyant cues
Keep Heels raised while head twirls to a stop a new
Eyes glare with a purpose at a compromised stature
Weights just shifted gently and it's a burn notice rapture,
Awkward slight aggression makes thought movement
slightly so increasing is the mighty
Light weights in flight musically controlled and beneficially brightly,
A smile is in toe while syllables flow with passion's presence
Upon multiple personas waiting intensely for isolation's gather
Adhere to the beat that keeps in time
Like a metronome corresponding to a click divine
Just like clockwork now flowing is mine,
Just like clockwork now easy is the atoning
To get back at me I'm so of the knowing
To get back at the muscle contraction like a beneficial cup of tea
That caffeinated calm that sore muscles complete
That caffeinated clam now muscles tinge with strength glee
It's a nonchalant strength so I'm now complete
Just heard a voice say to me no you're not complete!
This is a lifelong venture so stay alert my friend for the perpetual see...

Gratifyingly Appreciating

I'm not ready and it's too soon for butterflies are many
This sickness to my stomach is coo
I think I'll just slide to the side and abide
Watch while I jump in and jump out with workout comply
It's the majority of your presence that completes what I don't have in store
May I seek the soaking persona of knowledge galore
Experience steep and so complete
Readiness abounds
Bodies compound on and in step around
It's a cardio capacity and body build of astound
As I look around I see many of those sweating religiously
This crescendo of appreciating inside of me is a warm chill of glee,
Thanks to you for holding on while I hang to obtain
The information gathers of exercise no complain
Do you now see the tear of happiness elate?
Do you now see the smile that's been lingering for a while?
What about the laughter that came after the euphoric
happenstance abdominal admiring?
This gratifying of appreciating is appreciative awhiling…

Gratifyingly More

A sigh of relief as thankfulness does see
What was worked for over time with sweat excitingly
Staying alert of the times before and those to come
When modify is the demand to command an awkward stand of fun
Accommodation held to the high function
As aggressive appreciation is with so much comply
Reply to the create that keeps the embodiment abide,
A scan of the area upon faces of content
That are waiting on the next comparable exercise commit
Commitment perpetual is another exercise complete
Correct that now or a stand before thee by me I see
With smiles on me and sweat is all I see
The form was just corrected
Now on to the next
It's a repeatability,
Just like clockwork we're in unison
Reps mesh parallel with uniform's character
With a big smile now
I'm nigh to a sigh for joy exists omnipresent how...

Gratify Serene

Gazing over time and space upon multiple curvy souls
Unison minds contemplate a sweat worthy bodily control
Hands on hips
Heads turn briefly waiting on the instruction divine
A gleam in the eye of me dilates thankfully this time
Seen when they glance from each other to me
I smile,
One more rep I say as tensions flare to a flame for a while
Another rep is made as muscles blare to a bulge
Fibers tense to the point of an intertwined bundle of solidify indulge,
Releasing makes perfect of elongating quantify,
With a deep breath in thru the nose then out thru the mouth oblige
Exercise continues on as before
Stern looks of concentration isolates a reflect of feelings bold
I sigh
Years of butterflies in the stomach has made me appreciate why
Uneasy purposefulness had qualified for an abide,
Seconds pass and minutes do too
Appreciate continues with gratify approved
Perpetual endeavors calmly completes the present happy abode
Serene serotonin embodiment creates a clear implode
Now future thankfulness is omni present oh so and bold...

Pivot Plus

Load bearing leeriness lingers for real
Legs are sturdy still until arm twirl meets halfway appeal
Stop
Bend press and repeat the seat of forward progress
I see to my side an embodiment's surprise
Watch this squat worthiness of torso exercise
demise filled full of positive present
It's a stimulated presence with a smile for a while
That comes from exercised caressed candor flowing with a twist,
A workout of appeal
Knees near the floor from this plank position implore
Hamstrings are steadily engaged so a burning sensation is clearly at the door
Hamstrings scream no more
For movement soothes and strengthens too when
stand is upright confident and true,
Speed completes the cardio of sweat worthy body woes
Body twisting causes re-calibrate to take control now safety is so
Safely is a go into years of exercising cheers,
Pivot prove yourself transitional smooth
Until purpose additions is that of torque torso stabilized strong pursue…

A Boxer's Bend

I'm at a standing posture now
So press the gluteus down
Step back and stretch
Wiggle the feet until flat is set
Reverse movement commences then knees bends to a fast kick flex
Breathe out and snap
The movement is now a datum point kept correct
Mirror the burn that plagued the other leg
Isolation's positivity reclaims
A wide step shoulder shrug with width-wise on the mind
Makes a small bounce and bend of the legs gain power in and over time
Arms swing in unison combine,
A beneficial stretch is present when step back is once more
Lower than before the legs benefit from what's merely in store
A full extension of the muscle movement leads the
quest for optimum muscular improvement,
Sweat drops from the results of the squat kick and pop receiving provement
This dance is forever complete…

Perceivable Impact Ability

A floating feel it is when charismatic is for real
A warm-up to the fact when others seem surreal
I'll do and do and do it some more
Kiss you on the cheek until you adore
But will you do the same?
What happens when the times become so unbearable and so lame?
Change ability by the instigator just witnessed their game
Respond amplitude came closer and whispered to me your name
A constant realistic conspiracy of real knowledge meshed with wisdom
Remain and contain renders others' change ability insane tranquility
It's of exercise pertain so step back look and listen
Proceed and approach with caution less tear drops come near with fear
Wait a minute was that too much of a stop?
Let not me over compensate for others exonerated heart!
Time and time again renders tic toc proving well
The irritate that builds the knowing that time will soon tell
What has already been told if pay attention to detail is rightfully so
Open eyes in tow to yellow flags aglow
A wait until now makes yellow to red passionate so,
Deep breath is the prepare of it's now or never
Talk is no hesitate of yesterday's wear so contraire
is the contriteness of no say's aware
Say it like you mean it and no hold back of true
Heightened heart beats irregularly present anew
Deep breaths hyperventilated so now love is aware
Wind in eyes with a smile to the side makes perceivable that of compare
Brace for it now for you know of its abide
Wisdom now takes hold soothing no matter the woe wow…

Perceive Impact

So the day finally comes when benefits meets fun
When sweat meets happiness
A health happening for some,
Strategic endeavors
Wayside sleepers make room for dependency on dedicated committers,
Faith based caring for resulted heated benefited completed
When kinetic meets present
Then oh the presence of heat treated embodiment makes weakness depleted,
The tingling sensation of fibers inflated
Electric carriers precisely permeated
Now contour and shadowy are the sculptural praised
The impact of knowledge for the unknowable is amazed,
Optimized is the efficiency of time filled rationality
Esteem cared and focus aware
The multitude sternly staring studying this lifestyle comparing
And oh how they admire that dare to staring...

Flow Phenomena

With a jerk at the end of a modified movement
I witness a painstaking load jointly of needing improvement
Fast then slow is all the same
Repetitions awkwardness creates illusionary gain
Sets of supplementary uniquely forms keeping a witness of the same
Stubborn thought isms
Let not them lead to an embodiment detrimental,
Regroup the psyche and curl the ear lobes
Ready the musical for flow is the go
It starts in the mind
In the front of the eyes it hovers
The consequence of belief coupled with power-up energy endeavors
No jerk seen or conceptualized for fluent does
make the smooth movement perceptual
Sweat beads adorn smiling faces content
Innocent cardio goers seek benefits commit
No decent now for smooth depicts the groove that exercises
use to prove results blend sided achievable.
Cruise control is the flow of entertainments' endeavor
Charisma creates phenomena of nostalgia's' pleasure...

Scenic Surmise

Minutes before the event is about to start
I look across the room at the floor so empty
"It's quiet in here" I think to myself as I breathe easy
In just a few
Body movements will be in contempt just you wait and see,
I stand and stare into nothingness as meditation is aware to me
Heart rate quickens then slows
A thought of how a high-octane energy is about ready to create a woe,
The door handle moves now people do enter
Mats and weights depict the area to be exercise cantor
As they shuffle about, tensions rise awaiting for the potential kinetic surmise
So now music starts and so does the movement
The calm before the stormy beneficial chaotic in step remain provement
The conjure of sweat beads on bodies appease
A smile here and there depicts conditioning of please
A smirk then a smile
Says the burn makes me hate and love this
experience but only for a little while
Rest drink and presume I witness a resume
Cardiovascular isolation is a positive embodiment of consume
A look for the movement of chaotic disperse
Hold on let's do it now a regroup converse
Tweaking the tumbling of out of control exercise
Now we're in time and stepping in unison no surprise
This metronome madness is scenic of choreographed
and lovingly comprised…

Crenshaw Avenue

Going about my life at an earlier age and didn't
know what life was about to display
A fatherly fathom was forging a path in the mind
not soon to forget it's datings' datum
Creating a bond not known that it would be a brotherly fond
A working day to day with a smile for the bond
There's something more to life than the plain redundancy kind
Don't you see? He said to me
Yes, this is purpose but there's more at opportunity's store
Let's go get it he says but I'm reluctant more
Childhood scariness is clouding potentiality's
potentiometer now my vision is idle kind,
Still pitching the point of a monetary character and popularity's gain
Let's just try this once he says while my reply
contains convince with disorderly disdain
The belief that some came near from Atlanta's
abode to cause harm raised my alarm
So, I stay away conscientiously for the betterment of my blood pressure charm
That's selfish I now see and know, The hearing
from a far that it's a start slow
The steady to a hiccup for it's a Georgia gangster fault
Bodily infirmities have displayed that something is wrong
Too young to have an absentee report card that has already sung the song
Too young for no dream to occur the concur of this is much disdain for me sir
It's too late for me to be sorry but anyway I am
so please forgive me for the blurb
Why is my belief and knowledge base so far behind?

Why do I equate it to that of caught in time and
why is capitalize not the easy unwind?
I'll do what I can to make it up so here's to a
perpetual push contend in time…

Insanity's Happenstance

With a questionnaire glance from her
An inclination occurred from me in me
That an inquiring of something fitness related was surly about to be,
Hey have you ever performed an exercise of such?
It's high intensity internally let's give it a try of much
So much so I'm hoping for a no end result of die,
Walking thru the door I'm preparing in my mind
for an enclave of exercises intense of why
Let the music start!
She's looking at me with a purpose and I like it a lot
We're warming up to a sweat and she smiles
I like this plot a lot for no modify is not a why
I say to myself
Push to do more I say to her for you've been here before
Flow constant is what we do to the beat of the song
Thirty second approval repeat isn't a cardio capacity too long
This is a build of makeshift complete
This push sweating is aware and with us now
She smiles again with a stare of intrigue less the frown
Attractiveness is present with an eyebrow raise of glee
Push play and power up has come and gone now
more minutes are about ready to be
Cool down is an already contend until this next time of fun is done...

C 2 Internally

Internalize the endeavors to constantly contain
an energy efficient bodily remain
With Christ on the mind for a solitary sane
The reading content of wisdom was standing sustain
Converse to control the swerve of thought processes query remain
The thinking of efficient lifelong worthy embodiment better
What be the repercussions of an edible wreck less behavior?
What bombardment occurs timely absurd?
Eat to appreciate the energy's midriff levelized playing field blurb
ETA of cellular overheat depends on healthy conscience eating complete,
I look into your eyes,
I see a query demise
As I look into your demeanor it depicts 'A want for healthy but what's easier?'
Simple carbohydrates control the urge of energy's sub complete
Passionate the energy now and sublimate the meat
And so,
We pray for discipline coupled with physiology's integrity
And pray again for longevity's craving control…

Pine Needles Appreciable

Syllables heighten as the crescendo elevates
Flowing with ease it's a prepare for sedate,
Actions carried out with no care for the accident
Motivation is under the control of the alternate safety net
Subconscious is greater than me or thee
Don't you see how flow is perpetually a glee?
It's a nonchalant sip from the cup of honey tea
My body is a puppet under the influence of wisdom immense
Intuitive knowledge I call it a god sent,
Something's rising slow and steady for I can feel it constantly moving
In the middle it hesitates as if it's gaining some
sort of new knowledge of grooving
Oh, have you never felt it?
The contriving as the hippocampus flutters exciting the pineal
It's a euphoria of no absurd
Pineal is energizing so it summons a congregating
conglomeration of a hemisphere relating,
Euphoric passion is taking hold for I can sense
the full feeling fast approaching
Pine needles are bold as head tilts back with mouth wide open
A small scream is heard piercing eardrums imploding
Hands grab the side of the head as eyes squint with a bit of dread
The feeling of burst with tingling said
A surge remains as consciousness is super imposed,
And so, I appreciate now...

A Creek Wise Surprise

Sight sensitive the scenario from that of high-rise elegance
Witness the scene everglade serene
Meshed to the point of vegetation chaotic abstract
The look away then look back with a purpose so intact
Again the scenery is a rain forest akin
Water flows gently over the fallen trees that
decorate a seemingly troubled stream
Wind in eyes
Did you see the leaves turn over creating a new demise?
Squint then look again
Let not the wind make dry eyes a misconception of contend
The flapping of the leaves is a purposeful blend
Of yellow and green with a touch of red in between
One leaf falls abruptly like an amateur made paper plane
Now the witness is at your own risk for its disorder is supreme to blame
The rain now falls and I can see the landscape changing
The water that did flow gently down the stream now rushes with a rippling
It's a rising creek wise scene
The trees are covered more and the leaves are seemingly misplaced
I walk a couple of steps back then turn to the right
I go to another abide
The scenery I just left leaves me with a makeshift feeling of oblige,
The thoughts are present that I might sigh if again
Next scene is of a such surprising demise...

Executive Surmise

Hands gather the touch of plasticity smooth
After touching with multiple fingers there's a pause of purpose time true
Sliding into the slot of access gain
Walking through the door it's a deep breath ascertain
Peering from left to right it's a witness of impress that caresses
the sight sensitive leaving breath taking a success
Gliding from left to right now sitting on plush gray
Witnessing the theatrics of high definition maintain
On to the essential dinnertime debate
Extremities are a plenty it's a wood grain sedate
Aroma fills the overly spacious room while nose hairs tingle
Tongue licks the lips of aggressive as saliva inside the mouth builds
Stomach rumbles anticipating the fulfillment of a thrill...
Eyes are closed with the head laid back in a seat of much sit worthy
Feet are on the ottoman attached
Deep breathing in and out is the sound...
Meditation just induced the thin line between
no sleeping and sleeping abound...

Across the Tree Limbs Breezy

While standing and gazing I witness that these tall tree limbs are amazing
The sway of them quicken then slow to a mesmerize attaining
With wind in eyes a squint is now
Tenacious tears form to combat a withered brow
Hands grip the rail of a sturdy boundary travail
Heart beats slower believing safety is well,
Another peer over time into the horizon's sculptured sublime
Leaves me frozen
No wanting for this to unwind
Walking a few feet to the other side of this balcony proves
to be the same grandeur as the other side's pleasure
A raising to flash and preserve this awesomeness
by the way of cellphone madness
Two or three times prove no forgetfulness will come to this,
Pacing back and forth now with a stop in the middle
I look behind me to see if more people witness with glee
No voices or gestures meet me with an acquittal
To no surprise no one else does gaze at the size of this grand sight
But this does build wide eyes otherwise when some are told of this surmise…

Hiatus Creep

Nonchalantly relaxing into a state of appeal
That deals with lethargic being needful for real
Deep breathing is an anticipation of nerve endings soothe
The sound of deflating airways making one consequently coo
A deep breath to calm now breathing is constant
A flow of nervousness that decreases to Gnostic,
With back tracking a seem its really fast forward of a deem
Into clearness comparable it's a mystical dream
Of the crop keeping creative mindful splendid ream,
Must I go ahead the get into this land of meditative magnificent?
Must I care so much for the brain wavy tree of life commit?
The living of a life calmly and charismatic serene
Yes, I say yes while crawl to the walk run is bring
Standing with the gaze of amaze I look up around
Peering across the landscape it's more clearness astound,
Think I say think to grind the mind into wonder
Questions create questions answering answers of no blunder
The sound of air in and out of nostrils allow relax sleepiness about...

Push Prana

Clap the hands in commit
Straighten one arm overhead now bend the other in content
Side step that gaze now out of the corner of the eyes peer
Square up the embodiment
Sprint the intuitiveness while the knees pump faster in unison
Breathing lips are pursed in pursuit of passionate consecrating
Sweating is much ado
A concentrated stare is on the endeavor ahead
A dance mix of techniques makes the capacity enhancement efficient
Do you feel the comfort of cardio calmness?
It's time to push the passion
Do you feel the plush of the workhorses' saddle?
It's high time for the quarter horses' gaited push of matter
More energy to be used which was once on reserve
No conserve for now for benefits is on the verge
Of making one better enhancing cardio capacity crescendo
The strong thought process that survives life's stormy weather
Press the press of expedient no less for the milestone of next was just surpassed!
Are you impressed?
Breathe the breath of expanded lung capacity
The flourish of an enhanced life force commences...
Additional flourishes of independent's dependence...

Elevated Site Decent

This Euphoric feel is a cranium weightlessness
A grip of the hands meets seat belt tightness
Its tightness is a reassurance of no move able embodiment
As I peer out the window to my left I see clouds asunder moving slowly
My eyes witness patterns cotton like a blunder
Upon taking a deep breath my eyes witness a scene
Its wings hanging in the balance and shear is no dream
Shockingly I tremble now my heart is stable
The ground lies far beneath and I'm wondering how far when I'm able
To breathe even easier
Will safe meet secure from catastrophic decent?
A pray is now of no embodiment dement
A sip to soothe
Now a wait of subdue is fermentation's serene
This wetness calms my nerves of nervousness demean
Time has surpassed what fear has emboldened
Now courage remains to sustain a no complain molded
Reading makes dreaming commence to bypass
moments of chronic negative thought content
Pressure differentiate creates a euphoric confusion
Ears pop from a relative reach for a collusion balance of power
An inner hear is stabilize and stabilize is now ground worthy
The mind is now calm to a rest easy oblige…

Breath Aware

Hold still and listen
Now you hear it right?
The sound of hair follicles waving with time
The air that moves through them is of discipline's pleasure
How fast air moves is of euphoria's enhancer
A look to the left then straight forward in step
Listen becomes lookingly proud and strong kept
So
I breathe again to calm anxiety's storm
I breathe again to build sobriety's norm
One more breath to enhance meditation's worry
It's waging a war against society's aberrational scurry,
Nostrils flex as tempers flare from happenings of evil aware
I frown more at provocative actions that stand tall and stare
I stare back with no remorse
Breathing intensely and concentrated of course
Staying mindful of breaths in and out
This positive anger is fulfilling of wealth
I breathe again and brain waves comply to a frequency of creative surmise
Now the mind is stronger and the body is wiser exercising easy
Now wisdom is building and building is calm breathing
which leads to a much more aware…

Next Thought Needful

With thumbs interlocked and pointer fingers taping each other
They slow down then speed up as meditation's fire flickers
Head cocks to the side while the eye brows rise
A tickle inside the head makes me wonder of a mind's surmise
Seconds go by as through the nose breathing is ado
Eyes are closed now as eye lids gently move
A smirk to a smile proves a positive meditations' maneuver
Chin raises slightly as breathing does too
Eyes open to a squint as an abstract brainstorm churns wildly uncontrollable
Words whirl to and fro
A gather of unique word dance is playing with the mind's character
Let the words dance the mind says to me
Huh I say to myself
Let the words combine and dance to a rhythm
I just heard someone say?
Oh, wait that's me again
It's a perpetual begin
Calm the chaos you caring soul
Serene the sudden display of negativity bold
that is picking at the heart strands
That is staying strong for now
Diminish the destructive nature of a catalyst mind
Hmmm to idea's futuristic purpose
I'm waiting to know next thought's locality as
an involuntary clear is emerging...

Iris mediated

Positioned between those seeing with a conscious comply
It's seen only when the spirit mind is in line
With fine tune meditation
Visionaries are dilated
A wait in time for clearness is now unabated
Connected to the hemispheres of operation compilations hustle,
Now that's what you call a brain wave endeavor
With both eyes closed
The slight look up is impervious
Muscles in the eyes comprise of isolation's bulge
Witness the lightning strike admissible in darkness a bliss,
Another lightning strike now PG is equipped
With motivation to commence to an awaken commit
Super consciousness is a glimpse
A slight pop is felt and subliminally heard
Dizziness is consciousness regaining from a blur
Vibration awareness is of eardrum worthy remain
Constant says I'll retain vibrant until there's a beneficial complain
Thoughts conjure and flow with ease
The ability to pertain and describe is appease
Complying to life's everyday happenings it sounds so contrive
The more the journey continues the more one becomes alive…

Elevated and Mediated

A small glance up of the mind with a meditated combine
Euphoric tendencies are flirting with the divine
With eye lids closed the eyes are still wide open
Looking peering into a shape shifting appearing
The mind's eye sees what conscious can't entirely believe
All this coaxing has now created a spark to the flame of concurring
It pushes to the side the brain washing of society
It pushes to the side the brain wavy exoneration of dependent complacent
Spiritual elation is now serene allowing for no elevated alarm placement
This clear has created a push prana of admiration,
Head tilted slightly up
Can you feel the flourish of a tingling sensation?
Now up a little bit more
Can't you feel the nose hairs move gently?
Your deep breath is controlled and smooth into a soothe
As you breathe in you feel the diaphragm area move concurrently
Making no way for the air in there to remain pooling,
Abdominal area is witnessing a slender
Conscious concentrating breathing is a blender,
The euphoric created has now been mated with elevated
Its floating feel keeps the journey perpetually and
spiritually aiding with no complaining…

Saturated Prana

With the mind fixated on the thought process of breathing
Nose hairs tingling from the moment of constant air bringing
A through put of soothing
Diaphragm flexing
Chest expands as air inward is vexing,
Back arcs slightly as arms are extending
Head is tilted back and the mouth is open as an upward gaze is amending,
I feel a flourish of warmth euphoric comprise
A comprise of secular thoughts have brought spiritualistic arise...
A small pop around the medulla makes a smirk appear
Another pop and flourish it's a unity of left and right now the clear is near
A smile now completes what the smirk did smear...
Permeating and pulsating shoulders relax
Fingertips tingle with needle like feelings contract
There is now an extract from the interior to the exterior
The diaphragm flutters as root area is filled
A bloodletting sturdy comes near for real
On to the quads as knees shake to no shutter
Feet are planted firmly as toes tingle staying apart...
As eyes close a light appears
So bright so much it's a regal of tears
You know now that you've experienced a universe tingle event
Some have never imagined a thought of this dement...

Omni the Prana

Even before it's really ever known and even before the seed's been sown
From the depth of the soul's primitive DNA
The locked door is shaking to be opened and
it's ready for the urge to a display...
With a mind of its own connected to mine
It's communicating with me so I will listen
It's from the divine...
Days turn into years so reading is imploring for
more knowledge begets more questions
Oh no awake is in store ready for storing...
A ponder then wonder now permeate the meditate...
I just stumbled upon a realization
A new passion has met sedate now there's a peering through new eyes
A glorious surmise
More knowledge to understanding and less flourish of surprise...
This primordial presence can't you see it approaching?
Ancient knowledge is aware and universally caressing the character
The overshadowing of a presence so powerful and euphoric
Making one gasp for breath with eyes wide open deplorable
I'm craving for more in one accord...
Looking to the left and right along with up above and below it's there
The feeling of the chest about to explode makes one fearfully aware...
The permeating of the brain's hemispherical continue
Emanating from within after concentrating is akin...
The blinding radiance of euphoric tingle
The omnipotent eminence of timeless contentment
So great of an illumination it's like a feel of a deathly amendment
The spirit is now awake
So much so that omni makes a quake...

Mito Excels

A potential power up
Now lying in wait
Idle listic endeavors it is until needful is mate
Its bodily functions have consummated for its functions net
Worth is nonchalant in store of a momentous set...
Head explodes from a euphoric wow
The tingling pulsating makes hands grab it now
Mouth widens as a cry from me is heard
A tilt of the head constitutes an overwhelming positive oh well
The life force activity of thoughts in the brain
The mind now knows why hurting for so long has been a giant disdain
Membrane's memory exists to perform a tedious task
It's potentiometers' tachometer that says to stay on track
Let not lethargy mount an attack
On the brain in the brain causing more disdain
Pain even envy of those with motivated mitochondria remain
Jump start the process of activity continue intensity...
Ready the read ability and keep it careful until habit knows its longevity...

Pineal Gland Excite

Start the stare straight forward aware
Squint the eyes and look up you're there
The journey to stimulate DE-crystallize and necessitate
The gland that has been dormant for way too
long so be reactive enough to wait
When concentrated upon it'll be a stimulated pop of strong
A little bit of proactive
Do watch the perception be oh so super strong and collective
May it be that the calcified will not be so soon active...
Images appear apparent vivid and life like so what are they telling me?
Oh, it's just a heads up to be cautiously corrigible ...
Don't you see?
Concentration reveals a high octane of melanin
Sleep with me now fetal position positive for dream wearisome is purposefully
Eyes are twitching alpha state plausible...
The picture is now painted feminist ado true
What lies before my eyes but very please able construe...?
Pituitary gland be nice to me while you mate with pineal
Consummate is a glee...
Euphoria's flood is giving me a hazy like feel and I'm happy don't you see?
It feels as if I'm looking thru someone else's eyes
These ESP's are giving me a life changing surprise
So much so this picture is a monumental comprise...
Liquidized it is so crisp clear and concise
So, I breathe to achieve and appreciate for this break thru surmise ...

Push Weight

Grabbing the solid structure it's movable now
Time over matter has produced strength a wow
Frail so before
Now confidence is more when patience appreciated
compliance's present galore...
At this particular time
Bulk build is the wind
Intensity's threshold gut teeth unwind
Rest repeat and realize the comprise
Step thyself to the plate and take that deep breath
Oh my!
How euphoric has changed from before to nigh
Self-esteem supreme push more is redeem
Take a quick breath and push again
Wisdom makes time a beneficial personal win
For the step to the plate rendered add another plate
The conquered endured so add another plate
Until max becomes somewhat that of sedate
Scribble on the slate to remind and debate
Accomplishments can be obtained with no mate with break
Just a mate with unbreakable push more contemplate...

Push Knowledge

Reading seeking speed reading some more
Eyes pass over words to continue the explore
The implore to know to concentrate and show
First steps of reading easy starts with difficult in tow...
Now you're ready to pass it on
The trials and tribulations of obstacle words concepts and meanings
Which is to your advantage
May it propel you to an ultimate knowledge pursue...
Subliminal phrases projected at a contouring style sternly whispered
Crescendo compiled...
For a while a hiatus is kept with a smile
Even though a behind the scene workhorse spirit is wildly alive...
The emerge from the shadows
Observational tactic inserting phrases
Influencing static
Authority pragmatic
No hope for the underscore of ignorant tendencies
A bringing about a galore of intelligent actions positive more...
Pause for a second let's adore the elate of pushiness causality contour...

Push Wisdom

Energy primordial
A breath breathing portal
Learning leans to actions seemingly normal
Come on man it only costs this much
Which is not very much for you to pop the clutch
Of work hard to play hard of so very such
I'll wait while you keep that thought to your mind in touch...
Look how good it is when rationalization is combined with so much
Look how good it is when doing over and over is the commit crutch
Look at those outcomes so don't you just want to try them
Here's a taste
To savor the sweetness of this tongue tingling lip licking pleasure
Consequences correct to positive pleasing
More doing depicts efficiency teasing and it's so very aware
More knowing is now combined with this competitive compare
It's soaring past the congregations into parallel a stare
The more I do and repeat a loop the easier it becomes of intelligent continue...
The building of a skyscraper and it's projecting a symbol
Of weathered lines on a grimaced face
Lips are perched puckered as if a lemon has entered a tongue taste
Eyes are squinted into future's behold
Another knowing of how to know has became very bold...

Push Breathe More

Inhale to feel the capacity tighten of mid riff complexity
Follicles of the nose bend to filter the dust of life's impeccable muster
Eyes glare to the contrary of calm cool and collective
Red fiery aware is the stare into this aggressiveness
The start is a super push into longevity's non stop so don't you dare stop
Brain activity quickens after what is heard is a pop...
Now I'm driven
Hippo-campus is the mediator of the pineal no absurd...
Spirituality just got superimposed
Hadn't you heard?
The feeling is of a quicken so now is no perturbed...
Receptors flash to the tune of conceptual unlock
Synapses awaken to the music of no assume of block
Knowledge is being placed in line with an abstracted chime
Superconsciousness breathing bpm is so much sublime
Content is concise while constant is precise
Wave length is flowing with no spike of comprise...
Relaxed has been way too long so now push breathe strong
Push past comfort zones into that territory of belong
It's that territory of longevity's living fullness galore
Making one competitively excellent in life's value producing valour
Feet pounds the ground of speed worthy astound
No sound of pound for now float worthy is abound...

Subconscious Apotheosis

Breathing comparable to above comprising of able
Maneuver the obstacle of breathable growth recyclable
Vitality is now remembering longevity aware
Everything looks alive
Livable is at least a dare
Growth says it's time for perpetual death complete...
Rebirth is now multiple astound
Allowing a leaving to break free and gain ground...
With more cellular available new and improved
Communication is worthy while knowledge is building a clue of true
A creation of creativity and its pureness is you
Done so many times it's a second nature
Muscle memory completing so sleeping is a coo
Multiplying from dying is longevity's legacy
Gaining wisdom presently is DNA's passionate path
There's strength in numbers and time is a sensitive empath
I don't worry
No time is now for blunder's wrath blurry
Fist fight with meditation's tactical skill
Weave and connect bind with thought's perpetual appeal...
Positive has a purpose from a deathly trance
The chance increases more with a subconscious dance
Congregation's applause praises fertilization's stance...

Infinity's Advocate

Forever and ever there is no retreat
Forever and ever believe is the seed
Why does the belief get met with malice?
Why doth sadistic humanoids come near to impede the achieve?
With a blink of the eye
Stride is the comply
A moving past atrocities quick stepping to positive demise...
Keep pushing is the passionate sound of embodiment motivation
Flowing of this motivation keeps progression progressive
Propagandized blinky signs doth stimulate those hungry minds
They're waiting for that small push of congressional fortitude...
A look straight forward then up slightly
A stride then step faster now stronger is mighty
No maybe for greatly is not impeding or shady
I need and we need that unabating that pushes pacingly...
In case you encounter a non-motivating force
Embodied humanoids exercising lethargy of course
Exercise that quick thought of meditative
conscience creating positive producing
Uh oh
The value of thrive has just met with construe...
What a journey of positivity that's just came true
Steady the work of this so that this flow will continue ado...

To No Avail 2

The flowing constantly of loving so much
Movements depict that of video worthy such
From one flow to the next
It stays correct
The abstractness of upright posture so sweaty more is met...
Seems as if boring will come my way
Seemingly it's here can't you feel the display?
Of defacement face front dreary appear
Someone pushed play...
Then a push comes from somewhere else and its motivation's nourishment
To enhance the body and soul strength making it prudent
Pass it on says a voice coherently clear
Make this known lovingly entertainingly isolation near...
A flourish flows from head to toe
Tingling the follicles of sensation bold
One more time
Just one more
Then two more times were justified implore
They have just met sore a meaningful blissful bodily contour
Blessings come quickly when endurance is plural
Coupled with fun the optimized is won...
Never over it ever is
The combating of muscle tissue degradation explore...

Split Tree Sweaty

A quick look around the room as ready is made aware
Equipment is settled strategically
By congregational astound of compare
Commotion able syllables situate the mood of exercise able
likableness that's about to commence construe...
Focus depicts wait filled wistfulness wit of what's to come next true
Self-imponderable mate able of computational combination collect
The time has finally come for instruction correct
For a look around has seen structure undone
No worry for choreography caresses this dement with negotiating fun
The routine worthy of releasing stresses makes structure comparable a new
It's done...
Another look and I see it
It's knowing of no control nonchalant
Teaching touches my syllables showing them in tandem salute
No withdraw from this podium of spot light sweating shine
Let now thy bashfulness decline behind the veil of what was before
In your face proves the importance of technique critique
Breathe easy curvy one
Now resume your stature of continue
And complete with complacent of more fun...

Next Thought Possible

As I enter the room presenting presently I see quick looks with smiles
Tying shoes quickly now the snapping open of a CD case is the compile
It didn't take a while so push play is now...
Quick steps are in step and arms are pumping with pep
Power up is met now raise those knees too
Step to them then step the step away
Quicken the press in between as you set gluteus muscles in array
Stand and breathe now prepare yourself for repeat and complete
Two sets to three sets then isolate is the play
Two more sets let's correlate the muscle burn atrophy display
Till failure is a rewarding of positive complain
A second later the recovery does return and push is sedate
Marinade on these benefits we are now earning late
Let us breathe as this quick rest is a power recovery...
As I march a fingertip touches the temple
Thoughts of suppleness doth come very simple
A sought-after burn ratio of cardio is isolation's purpose
On you in you as benefits continue to show its ultimate contour
No ignorance here although the cup does run over
of that which contains much bliss...
Another fingertip touch to the temple and the
tap is to the forehead center now
Thoughts twirl around concepts made before concentration implores...
A perpetual contemplation is now...

Perpetually Inconcludable

The actions contained
Strategic movements to blame
The repeatable obtainable isolation able momentarily complain
A pull out of the easel
Script scribble concentrate able
A blueprint to enhance the body is now very conceivable
The date has been noted to deepen the perception able
Daily usage by many makes surface the collection
Used so much plateau has challenged for a correction
The connection has made skin muscular bumpy and stiff hairy a tingle
This has made body sweats from heat breathing a mingle
So,
I breathe and we breathe...
Another action contained is a blend
Strategic wanes is of a makeshift sin akin
A deep breath then legs flutter and sweat particles fly to and fro
This is from a decompressing of lung capacity efficiency so...
What happens is push perpetuals of weight training essentials
This hurt is muscle aching and soothing consensual
Movements exponential is a body full feeling of tightness and correlation
Bodily contour mirrors the sight way more than slightly affectionate
Perpetual makes us forever plateauing proud...

Accumulative Acclimation

Cylindrical twisty and intertwining bound
Strategic movements make way for strength astound
Elasticity proven
Lengthy is the student
When teachable tactics are studied passionate
Time renders a chiseled structure magnificently prudent...
Started from the seed of knowledge being planted at random
Wanted nonchalantly from seasonal of chime
The growing proceeds from nutrients of time
Once thought that a happening would never be this bliss
The happenstance of this is everyday a dreamy kiss
Benefits of a bodily
Heart healthy too
When projected upon others the smile turns to
laughter a much needed pursue
Didn't thou just witness a clue?
Longevity pursue is due and paid instantly true
Its fun is a rendering of remembering for years have begun
And are continuing
For faith hath found getting fit a snug bit of fit
What fabric is now this cloak of commit?
What accumulation hath led to this wardrobe
of fashionable acclimated style?

Foresight Achieving

Peering forward into the abyss
It's fitness' positive and this is not a miss
Don't you fret one moment even though face front presently is wane
There's coming a time soon where no complain is claim,
It seems as if I'm about to complain for I don't feel the strength of strong,
The length of this stride just lengthened for the pursue of strengthening true
Time over time renders benefits a new,
The exertion of my energy just met a wall
I can only see from here to a few feet ahead
That's all
I feel as if I'm trying so hard and that it can't get easier than this
When will the time come when completion becomes a bliss?
Incremental additions to an eagerly steady stride
Here it is now
The worthy wordplay of push forward array
Combine that with perseverance renders a
readiness of enhancement pursue in play
I'm now exerting the same and the results are better
Time has proved once again the ultimate relapse
of the muscle memory positive letter
The monument milestone appears larger and larger
as creeping closer it becomes apparent…

Screamingly Retreating

What syllables were said to go right ahead?
What truth truthiness just flowed with hot dread?
Nonchalant and calm just reared a heavy head
With a touch of sincere the pierce did come near
Poking at obscurities creating a beneficial clear
To me at least and what a beast it was
The enduring of screaming choice bleeping for sure
The night just enhanced the makeshift maturities to be immature allowing
The leading of youthful curious was just made aggressively loud
Don't come at me with choice word
Watch what thou lips utter for kids are near to learn
Made at me I do see for truth hurts the clouded heart
Brutally it is so whats wrong with it?
A decent projection of life's face front movie
It's more about them you just said
Flippy flop was the epitome of actions proving
That practice the preach was obscured and surprisingly compromised
As I lay here I think unto myself and wonder
Why must one perform acts and reacts of asunder?…

September 2 2015

I'm driving towards a city so what city is it?...
I'm in a speed boat now
Wind in my eyes are of the demise
Nighttime now is of the comprise
The mouth of this waterway is the precinct of an Orleans surprise
To my left? but I go right
Now I'm peering at a majestic waterfall in close sight
I can see water rushing over the side of the hill as I approach the drop off
A rock formation suddenly comes up out of the water just inches from me
I grab hold
The speed boat is no more as I'm carried higher still by the rock formation
I'm way up in the air now
Looking down to my left i can see how shallow the water is in places
Same as on my right
Interestingly enough I'm still close to the waterfall drop off
I see the night lights of New Orleans
Feeling great fear it quickly goes away
I jump down from the rock formation toward a shallow area in the water
I plunge toward the water with wind in eyes
I'm in the water now having felt no impact...
I'm climbing out on dry land
A man of creole comes to me and asks me if I
have received my parents' luggage?
I say no and we talk for a while...

January 13-2018

It's daytime and all the snow has melted…
I'm standing in a warehouse
Multiple people are around
They're about six feet apart
A Music video is a likely astound
One guy is close to me in shiny blue suit
He's staring at me with a sinister grin
This warehouse is full of pillars now
with lots of windows akin…

January 21-2018

Standing in my kitchen
The back doorknob is rattling
No fear at this time is a part of my heart chattering
To the woman sitting at my kitchen table I declare
"I'll just open the door and see who's rightfully there"
She just said to me
"Go ahead and do it now"
As I open the door I see that a woman is standing there
She summons to me to follow her
Following her across my yard I stop before walking out into the road…
I'm returning to my house now…

November 21-2018

I'm in a policeman uniform carrying a shot gun
This grocery store parking lot walking is not a lot of fun…
Walking toward the entrance now and I see a gray mustang
That used to be owned by a good friend NE
Did you just think about drinking a Tang?
Geez
Looking to my right I can see just inside the door
The getting of a latte renders a blind sight implore…
There's someone in a nearby tree just across the road
My shot gun is pointing at them
There's about to be an implode…

January 17-2019

Immediately after walking through a doorway
My feet almost touch a rushing river…
We are floating on this ship that's just a couple of feet over the water
I see what looks like snakes swimming around
wooden stakes in the water
When the snakes see us they dart under the water
They emerge seconds later…
Still floating above the water I suddenly feel a gripping fear
We are floating higher now
Submarine?
Someone is shooting wooden logs at us!
I can now see the doorway that we came through earlier
As we get closer to the door I start to feel better
Going through the door I look back to see it closing
One last log is being shot as us…

January 18-2019

This is the second time…
I hear commotion going on outside…
Going through some glass doors
Why am I walking into the library of congress?
I'm standing in this empty room with no chairs or a counter
After looking around for a while I leave…
Walking back into the room now multiple people
are standing around and talking
I turn right around and some of the people are instantaneously gone
I wonder where they went?
Frustrated I leave quick then storm back through the doors
As I scan around the room I see a small opening in the wall
Pushing the wall gently it slides around and I see a hallway
As I walk through I look behind me to see that no one is following
Opening the door at the end of the hall proves to be magnificent
A huge library lies before me lined with books and books
My mind and eyes are full of looks
I see computers with screen savers moving
A librarian is at her desk
I see people sitting around the room studying
The most joyful feeling ever fills me…
Walking down the hallway to leave I think unto myself
I'll be back soon…

May 30-2019

I'm standing by a freeway on this bridge
TS is standing to the left of me and TL is on my right
TL is smiling
I can feel the wind from the vehicles zipping past us
We are standing dangerously close to the road
A concrete pillar is obstructing our view just to the right of TS
A wall is just beyond the pillar
I step out onto the road a couple of feet to see if a car is coming
I just get out of the way
This happens two times
TS steps out one time for good measure then calmly walks back to me
I walk out into the road all the way to the other side without hesitation
TS joins me and gives me a kiss
TL is standing on the other side of the freeway laughing at us...

June 20-2019

I'm standing outside with a male figure
We see a UFO hover very close to the ground
I am alarmed
The UFO is hovering over McDonald's now
More smaller UFOs appear much higher up in the sky
We are standing in the grass next to Wendy's
Why are there trees where the UFO almost landed?
The trees were not there before
A wall of fire from the UFO hits the area of
McDonald's so we take cover...
Emerging what is seen is like a war zone
The building known as Wendy's is partially destroyed
As we walk toward McDonald's we see buildings charred and smoldering
The whole area has been devastated
We see the remains of charred bodies and the
building known as McDonald's is no more
I say" the earth has been burnt with fervent heat"
I feel much sorrow as the thought in my head persists
"I hope they don't return"...
Me and this woman are standing outside beside a building
We see UFOs approaching from a distant
We run to the back of the building with anticipation of an attack
She starts taking off her shirt and directs me to do the same
Oh no! The US President has just wired the door shut with explosives
We crawl through a small hole in the wall to enter the building
I see a man lift a manhole cover
I walk over to him and command him to hold my plate of food?
The woman crawls through the manhole first
Crawling through the hole I look up to see the UFOs strikingly close...

May 30-2021

I'm riding my bike down the main road in the middle of double yellow lines
I can feel the sun beaming on my head...

Walking in this room
I stop by a table with people eating drinking and talking in the dark...

September 5-2021

I'm in the front yard of a big white house
I've been here before
I see three cages with lions in them
The last time I was here there were only two cages
In the first cage it is riddled with female and male lions
The second cage has the same
In the third cage there are two lions one male and one female
I notice that the fences surrounding the cages are about four feet high each
Eyeing the third cage I see the female lion with
her front paws on top of the fence
Oh no now she has her back paws on the fence with the front two in the air
I am now very alarmed
I look beyond the cages and see two picnic tables
with people sitting and eating at them
I can't go to the people for the cages are too close
together for me to pass between
Going around to the back yard I encounter another cage
There are chickens an old dog and an armadillo in it
I look around to the front yard to see the female
lion from the third cage leap out
Afraid I stand by the cage in the back yard preparing to run in the house
I hear the old dog whimper as the armadillo stands
still, it's skin shining from the sun
The lion is walking from around the opposite end of the house toward me...

About the Author

After being born in Indianapolis IN, there was a quick move to Burkesville Ky where Jason grew up and graduated in 1993.

He was a graduate of Kentucky Advanced Technology Center in Bowling Green Ky in 1995.

His residency is now in Glasgow Ky where it has been since 1996.

At 46 years of age, his primary work includes that of a Research and Development Technician at Tenecco where he has been employed for 24 years.

It has been an enjoyment being an Employee/Fitness Instructor and Personal Trainer at the Barren County Family Ymca for 23 years.

May the look/correction inside yourself be a positive penetration....

Jason's previous works of poetry include:

Transcendental
Religional Ties
Love Strands
Dream Innovatively

Printed in the United States
by Baker & Taylor Publisher Services